FROGS

Edited by Danielle J. Ibister
Printed in China

00   01   02   03   04   5   4   3   2   1

Library of Congress Cataloging-in-Publication Data available

ISBN 0–89658–456–9

Distributed in Canada by Raincoast Books, 8680 Cambie Street, Vancouver, B.C. V6P 6M9

Published by Voyageur Press, Inc.
123 North Second Street, P.O. Box 338, Stillwater, MN 55082 U.S.A.
651-430-2210, fax 651-430-2211

Educators, fundraisers, premium and gift buyers, publicists, and marketing managers: Looking for creative
products and new sales ideas? Voyageur Press books are available at special discounts when purchased in
quantities, and special editions can be created to your specifications. For details contact the marketing
department at 800-888-9653.

Page 1: Red-eyed tree frog
Page 4: Bullfrog

FROGS

Text by David Badger
Photographs by John Netherton

WORLDLIFE
LIBRARY

Voyageur Press

Contents

The Fundamental Frog

Frogs are truly marvels of nature. They may lack the hair, feathers, fins, and scales of their fellow vertebrates, but they possess remarkable skins—vividly colored, smooth (or warty), permeable to moisture, and often loaded with powerful toxins. What's more, their eyes look like jewels, their voices resonate like bullhorns, and their limbs and feet can be mobilized for hopping, leaping, walking, swimming, digging, climbing—even gliding through the air.

Frogs and toads (the latter are technically frogs, too) are amphibians, styled as such not because they constantly shuttle back and forth between land and water but because most begin life as aquatic larvae (tadpoles) "and later change shape and go out on land to live," herpetologists Archie Carr and Coleman Goin explain. (Salamanders and tropics-dwelling caecilians are also amphibians, while snakes, lizards, turtles, crocodilians, and tuataras are reptiles.)

According to recent estimates, there are about 4,360 species of frogs worldwide—a number that increases each year with the discovery of new species. Frogs can be found on every continent except Antarctica, though they are absent from a number of isolated islands and Greenland. Their widespread distribution is remarkable because, unlike "warm-blooded" (endothermic) birds and mammals, frogs are "cold-blooded" (ectothermic). That doesn't mean their blood is cold, of course, just that at any given moment their internal body temperature is within a few degrees of the ground or air temperature. A few species, such as African sedge frogs, bask in sunshine to boost their body temperature, but that behavior is more typically associated with reptiles than amphibians.

Like many mammals, frogs that live in regions subjected to cold temperatures hibernate during the winter. In areas that are unusually hot or dry, however, certain species "estivate," or retreat underground, and some, such as the water-holding frogs of Australia, prevent moisture loss by surrounding their bodies with cocoonlike layers of shed skin. At least four North American species (wood frogs, spring peepers, chorus frogs, and gray tree frogs) are now known to survive subfreezing winter temperatures by manufac-

The bright colors of South America's yellow-banded dart-poison frog (Dendrobates leucomelas) *warn predators of this species' dangerous skin toxins.*

turing a sort of "antifreeze" and suspending their heartbeat.

Over the last two centuries, herpetologists—the scientists who study reptiles and amphibians—have engaged in numerous public brawls over the nomenclature and classification of frog species and subspecies. Today, most recognize about twenty-eight families of frogs, including tree frogs (770 species), the so-called "true" frogs or ranids (650 species), "true" toads (400 species), dart-poison frogs (more than 170 species), and a large assortment of other unusual families and species.

The sedge frog of eastern Africa often sunbathes on cool mornings for hours at a time to boost its body temperature.

By whatever scientific or common names, these tailless amphibians are hardly the "foul and loathsome" beasts that the Swedish scientist who coined the term *Amphibia* more than two hundred years ago made them out to be. In fact, frogs have become highly popular, even idolized, in recent years. Frogs are television and film stars, storybook heroes, family pets, and environmental icons, featured prominently on posters, T-shirts, computer software, advertisements, toys, and even wine labels. But as celebrated as Kermit the Frog, Michigan J. Frog, the Budweiser bullfrogs, Peace Frogs, Flumpa, and various tourism symbols have become, it is the shocking evidence of severe declines in frog populations, the extinction of several species, and chance discoveries of thousands of deformed specimens in more than thirty states and Canada that have generated the most significant media attention.

It is now painfully obvious that if we want future generations to enjoy this planet's wondrous assortment of frogs and toads, we must better understand their physical characteristics, reproductive behavior, and habitat requirements. We must also identify and halt practices that are degrading, even destroying, the environment around us.

Paradoxically, frogs are often revered by humans for the same physical attribute that makes them so highly susceptible to external environmental threats: their skin. Frogs typically have smooth skin, while most toads have rough or warty skin—although the reverse can be true as well. Frogs and toads are dressed in a remarkable array of colors, and in Central and South America, tree frogs alone embrace "the entire visible spectrum," says one expert. The brightest colors are characteristically associated with the most dangerous species—those that secrete deadly toxins, such as the dart-poison frogs—or their mimics. Vivid reds, yellows, oranges, blues, and other gaudy hues are called "aposematic," or warning, colors; their adaptive purpose is to signal predators to keep their distance. Also common are the greens, browns, tans, dull grays, and spotted patterns—the "cryptic" (concealing) coloration of many species, including North American green frogs, wood frogs, gray tree frogs, leopard frogs, and most toads. Some species boast a curious mix: cryptic colors on their back for camouflage and vivid "flash colors" on the underside or flanks to startle predators. Two examples are the fire-bellied toad, which has a dark-green back and bright-orange underside with black spots, and the red-eyed tree frog, which is neon green with blue or purple stripes on its flanks.

During periods of drought, the water-holding frog of Australia burrows underground, where it sheds its outer layer of skin to create a "cocoon" that inhibits moisture loss.

The skin secretions of many frogs and toads can be highly irritating, or even toxic, to humans. Some species can paralyze a dog that clamps its jaws around one of these creatures, and dart-poison frogs are used by some South American natives, who apply the frogs' skin secretions to blow darts to immobilize or kill prey.

Other glandular secretions can lubricate a frog's skin, prevent excessive evaporation, and protect against bacteria and viruses.

The beautiful skin colors of frogs are rivaled by the dazzling colors of their eyes. Many frog eyes have bronze- or copper-colored irises, and others bear gold or metallic flecks. (Shakespeare refers to a toad that wears "a precious jewel in his head" in *As You Like It*.) Also intriguing are the pupils—usually horizontal, sometimes vertical, and occasionally round, triangular, or diamond-shaped.

As a rule, the body shape of a frog differs a bit from a toad's: The latter is more often squat with shorter legs, better adapted to short hops than to long leaps. Many frogs and toads use their front legs like hands to stuff a stubborn or oversized insect into the mouth, but it is their hind legs that provide the real strength. Powerful muscles in the hind legs of "true" frogs, such as bullfrogs and leopard frogs, propel them through the air and help them to evade predators— including humans, who are partial to the succulent hind legs served at gourmet restaurants and French bistros. A bullfrog's hind legs enable it to leap up to nine times the length of its body, though the tiny Southern cricket frog tops that by jumping a whopping thirty-six times its body length. When startled, a wary green frog or bullfrog will catapult itself toward nearby water, straightening its legs and closing its eyes and nostrils when diving. The frog then swims in true "frog kick" fashion by drawing its well-muscled hind legs up close to the body, then thrusting its well-designed webbed feet outward.

The cryptic coloration of the North American gray tree frog conceals this species when it clings to rough bark and lichen on trees.

Frogs are able to move in a variety of ways: They can walk, run, hop, leap, dive, swim, climb, dig, even "fly." Climbing is surely one of their more spectacular feats, made possible with adhesive disks found on the toes of tree frogs. These toe pads are enlarged and sticky from mucous secretions, permitting the tree frogs not only to climb straight up a tree and onto leafy bowers but also to maintain a hold on vertical glass and walls, where surface tension ensures adhesion. On summer nights in North America, gray tree frogs and green tree frogs often turn up on windows, attracted to insects lured by the light. Another spectacular feat is the "flying" or gliding of several tropical tree frogs in Southeast Asia. These so-called "flying frogs" descend from treetops by spreading the broad webbing of their front and hind feet and "parachuting" to lower branches or to the ground.

In addition to well-muscled hind legs and unique toe pads, frogs have another distinctive physical characteristic: a pair of round, bulging eyes. These eyes offer a remarkable field of vision—the most extensive of any vertebrate—and quickly detect moving predators and prey. Because a frog's vision is somewhat farsighted, an object directly under its nose may be harder to see than one several feet away. A frog employs its long, sticky tongue to snatch live prey and to yank it back into the mouth. Unlike the human tongue, which is attached at the back of the mouth, the amphibian tongue is anchored at the front and points inward; when snapped into action, the tongue of some species (especially toads) can flip out a good 2 inches (5 cm) or more.

Chorus frogs emerge from hibernation early, sometimes even in winter, and sing in large choruses. They survive subfreezing temperatures by manufacturing glucose that functions like antifreeze.

Some frogs actively search for food, while others sit and wait for prey to come to them. The Argentine horned frog, for example, buries itself in leaf litter on the forest floor and engulfs its victims—including mice and small birds—in its huge jaws. Like all frogs, this Neotropical species (nicknamed the "Pac Man frog") is carnivorous, swallowing its prey live and whole. Some species of horned frogs even dangle their hind legs over their head and vibrate their toes to lure prey into range.

Most frogs have tiny teeth on their upper, and sometimes lower, jaws, though this is generally unnoticed by humans; toads, however, usually lack teeth altogether. Unlike mammals, frogs do not "chew" their prey; instead, their teeth hold prey in place to prevent it from escaping. On many a dark summer evening, I have watched a green tree frog eagerly gulp down a lightning bug, an insect rejected by other species of frogs apparently due to its bad-tasting chemicals; before the bug expires, however, it continues to flicker for a minute or two, lighting up the tree frog's throat and belly with its glow. In tropical Asia, the teeth of one unusual species, the so-called fanged frog, are so large they protrude from the lower jaw.

A frog's sense of smell is relatively insignificant for food recognition, though the strong odor of algae may provide an olfactory cue for a frog or toad, helping it to return year after year to the pond where it was born. Hearing, however, is very important to a frog, particularly when a sound is accompanied by a visual stimulus. Most frogs and a number of toads have a prominent round eardrum, called the tympanum,

The Argentine horned frog conceals itself in leaf litter on the forest floor and waits for prey to come within range of its huge jaws.

situated behind the eye. The tympanum responds to sound stimuli and transmits vibrations to the inner ear. Frogs are able to distinguish the calls of their own species (each species has its own unique call), so vocalizing and hearing are essential to locating a mate for breeding. Many frogs have a prominent vocal sac that puffs up like a small balloon and resonates the sound of the frog's call after air passes over the vocal cords in the larynx. Scientists at the University of California–Los Angeles have recently reported that the tympanum also functions as a "boom box" or loudspeaker, amplifying the frog's vocalizations.

Whether performing solo or in large ensembles, frogs and toads have earned quite a reputation as some of nature's most gifted musicians.

Vivid "flash colors" on the underside of the Oriental fire-bellied toad may startle predators and warn of highly toxic skin secretions.

Musicians of the Night

"Frogs do for the night what birds do for the day: they give it a voice," naturalist Archie Carr once observed. "And the voice is a varied and stirring one that ought to be better known." Carr cherished the pleasing "swamp songs" of his native Florida, but he also recognized that "perhaps the reason frog songs are not generally appreciated is that they are sung in places where mosquitoes and snakes live."

The musical repertoires of frogs easily rival those of birds in their richness, variety, and beauty. Although many humans characterize the calls of male frogs as "croaks" or "ribbitts," the sounds are far more diverse, incorporating snores, grunts, trills, clucks, chirps, buzzes, rings, whoops, whistles, growls, quacks, and various other noises. In the American Southeast, for example, the pig frog grunts like barnyard swine, the barking tree frog yaps like a hound, and the carpenter frog sounds like "two carpenters hammering nails slightly out of synch," authority Lang Elliott reports. Numerous other species, such as the sheep frog, bullfrog, squirrel tree frog, cricket frog, chirping frog, and spring peeper, acquired their common names through their distinctive vocalizations.

One herpetologist recalls a memorable episode from his childhood when his mother was playing chamber music with virtuoso Fritz Kreisler at home and suddenly the youngster's pet tree frogs chimed in—"to the amazement and annoyance of the great violinist." Yet such a response from male frogs is not all that unusual: Bullfrogs sometimes sing when they hear airplanes overhead, and other frogs may react to sirens, whistles, trains, fire engines, construction equipment, orchestras, or nearby choral groups. (One of my own green tree frogs sounded off regularly when he heard our washing machine running, and he also voiced his throaty *quank-quank-quank* in response to a neighbor's car alarm, a popcorn popper, our dog lapping water from her dish, Scott Joplin ragtime music, and cannons in the Civil War movie *Gettysburg*.)

Scientists have identified about a half dozen or so different types of frog calls. The best known is the advertisement call, performed by males during the breeding season to signal their species, sex, location, and readiness to mate. Some males perform solo, while others sing in giant choruses (up to 1,000 frogs or

The inflated vocal sac of a male green tree frog resonates to attract a mate, announce an impending rain shower, or respond to loud noises such as car alarms and washing machines.

more), which are audible more than a mile away. Beginning in late winter or early spring, depending on the region and climate, and extending into the summer, waves of mating calls from different species fill the air—usually, though not exclusively, after sundown—as more and more sexually mature males emerge from hibernation and direct females to the breeding site. The volume of sound generated by a chorus

The pig frog is a large aquatic species that grunts in choruses and sounds like a farmer's swine.

benefits males and females alike, since widely dispersed females can locate a large assemblage of males more easily—particularly the "explosive breeders," which engage in "scramble competition" for mates in temporary pools of water created by heavy rains or melting snow.

Interestingly, a chorus of high-pitched spring peepers singing their distinctive *pe-ep, pe-ep, pe-ep* is not just a discordant rabble of frogs sounding forth at the same instant but, rather, sets of trios, naturalist Olive Goin discovered. "One frog starts things off by sounding the note A, [which] stimulates another frog to respond with a G#, and the two call back and forth. . . .

Now the last member of the trio chimes in with a B, and so they continue: A, G#, B . . . , a full chorus of many of these tiny independent trios."

The vocalizations of other species are equally distinctive: the deep bass *jug-o'-rum, jug-o'-rum* of the bullfrog, the unnerving *waaaaaah!* of the Fowler's toad (which some New England settlers likened to the sound of a band of Indians), the *cack-a-hack-a-hack* of the wood frog, and the *ribbitt, ribbitt* universally heard in Hollywood movies to enhance the "atmosphere" of Southern swamps and African jungles alike, even though the call belongs exclusively to one species, the Pacific tree frog.

A second recognized vocalization is the release call—a sharp chirping sound made by a male mistakenly clasped by an overly enthusiastic male in search of a female. Another vocalization is the distress call, a loud cry or scream voiced when a frog has been seized by a predator, such as a snake or bird, intended to startle the intruder and cause it to drop its victim. Some territorial species, such as bullfrogs and gray tree frogs, also utter the aggression, or encounter, call, which signals the anticipation of physical contact.

Barking tree frogs blend well with their arboreal surroundings. Their name refers to their raucous houndlike yapping sound.

The squirrel tree frog, sometimes called the rain frog, produces a raspy rain call that sounds like the chattering or scolding of a squirrel.

Other frogs, such as green frogs, have developed an alarm call, which they sound when they detect an intruder—often as they are leaping to the safety of nearby water. Some tree frogs and other nonaquatic species also produce a raspy rain call in humid weather or just before a rain shower.

Males of a few species—such as the tailed frog of the Pacific Northwest and Canada and the striped mountain toad of South Africa, both of which live in fast-moving water—have no voices at all. Although most female frogs are mute, those of several species can produce aggression sounds if provoked.

When singing in large choruses, spring peepers produce a deafening, high-pitched din, audible at distances of a mile or more.

While some frogs sing by day, most begin crooning after dark, much to the irritation of their human neighbors. During the Middle Ages, servants were sometimes hired to throw stones into ponds at night to silence frogs that made too much racket, and during the French and Indian Wars, the residents of one small Connecticut village fled their homes when they mistook the sound of an "army" of frogs for enemy soldiers. In Britain, where the edible frog and marsh frog are "the noisiest species we have," herpetologist Malcolm Smith reports, nighttime concerts by these frogs "have roused whole villages to indignation."

To achieve this arresting acoustical feat, males pump air back and forth over their vocal cords into a loose pouch of skin called a vocal sac. American toads and tree frogs characteristically inflate a single balloonlike sac in the area of the throat, while other species have throat sacs that bulge outwardly on both sides or that inflate near the shoulders. Experts who have recorded the songs of a single species of frog in more than one locale have detected variations, or "dialects," among these voices.

"A New Jersey cricket frog, clicking away very much as crickets do, makes a sound slightly different than a South Dakota cricket frog does," authority Flora Douglas reports. And when a female New Jersey cricket frog is confronted with simultaneous performances of recordings of males from both populations, she will be attracted to the vocalizations with the New Jersey dialect.

The throat of a male Blanchard's cricket frog often turns bright yellow in the spring.

The calls of most North American frogs and toads, originally recorded by field researchers, are now available on audiotapes and CDs, making identification of different species much easier than before. One popular recording is Lang Elliott's "The Calls of Frogs and Toads: Eastern and Central North America" (1992); in 1998, Smithsonian Folkways's re-release of Charles Bogert's classic 1958 recording, "Sounds of North American Frogs," popped up on music charts, despite some confusion over just which musical category the frog performers belonged in.

The repertoires of all these tiny musicians—who sing their songs underwater, on land, and from the treetops—not only produce a rich diversity of sounds but also evoke tributes from famous authors. The Greek playwright Aristophanes incorporated the sound of a chorus of European edible frogs into his satire *The Frogs* (405 B.C.), and John Steinbeck wrote nostalgically of frogs on California's Cannery Row, recalling (in his novella of the same title) that "there were frogs there all right, thousands of them. Their voices beat the night, they boomed and barked and croaked and rattled. They sang to the stars, and to the waning moon, their beloved love songs and challenges."

In the spring and summer, the Fowler's toad utters a mournful cry that sounds like a herd of calves or a band of wailing children.

Life Cycle of a Frog

The serenade of the male frog is, in reality, an overture to the act of amplexus—the mating embrace in which a male clasps a female from behind and fertilizes her eggs externally. Males of many species actively seek out a mate, and some, in their frenzy, mistakenly clasp another male (or perhaps a dead fish, floating debris, or an observer's boot). After fertilizing the eggs, the male moves on in search of another female. To arouse a mate, females of some species must first nudge the male. Some females are apparently attracted to particular mates by the quality (duration, pitch, or volume) of their lusty vocalizations.

Most frogs, though by no means all, spawn in water, where the transparent jelly that protects the eggs absorbs moisture and swells. Some egg clusters form huge masses that spread across the surface of a pond; others become compacted into globular clusters and attach to underwater plants. The fertilized eggs of other frog species are deposited on the ground, in damp leaf litter, muddy nests, or water-filled bromeliads. Clutch sizes can vary considerably—from the single egg of the Cuban tree toad, believed to be the smallest frog in the world (it averages about three-eighths of an inch, or 1 cm), to as many as 35,000 laid by the cane toad—a bulky behemoth that grows up to 10 inches (25 cm).

As the single cell of a fertilized egg undergoes repeated division, the yolk provides nutrition for the developing cells. The rate of development varies, depending on the water temperature, rate of evaporation, and other factors. Spadefoot toad larvae, for example, can develop in two days in deserts where rain puddles evaporate rapidly, while the eggs of other species in permanent bodies of water may take several weeks. By the time the larva emerges from the egg, it has assumed the familiar tadpole shape: large head, small eyes, and a filmy, elongated tail. As the larva develops, relying initially on external gills, it scavenges on plants or decaying matter using rows of tiny toothlike denticles inside its horny beak.

The metamorphosis from tadpole to frog may take only a few days, depending on such variables as population density and food availability, or, in the case of the bullfrog, the change may take two years or longer. Rear legs are the first limbs to become visible, followed by the front legs. The tail eventually shrinks,

During metamorphosis, a froglet such as this red-eyed tree frog continues to exhibit a tail until it has been fully absorbed into the body.

absorbed from within, and as the transformation nears completion, the still-tailed creature can be seen emerging from the water for brief periods of time.

Not all frogs conform to this standard model of reproductive behavior, however, and some exhibit remarkable diversity. For example, foam-nesting frogs in Africa, Asia, and Mexico whip up a communal

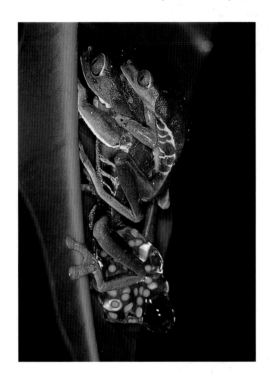

A male red-eyed tree frog climbs onto the back of a female and fertilizes her eggs as she deposits them on the underside of a leaf.

meringuelike froth that hardens around the eggs and protects them in their leafy nursery, suspended over a body of water. As the tadpoles develop, the foam gradually dissolves and the tadpoles slide down into the water below. Their descent is similar to that of the red-eyed tree frog of Central America, whose life cycle, from fertilization of the eggs through metamorphosis from tadpole to tree frog, has been recorded on film by photographer John Netherton.

Male red-eyed tree frogs call from the heights of trees in tropical rain forests, where their activity begins around sunset. Anyone who has ever kept one of these frogs in a terrarium has probably noticed its reluctance to engage in typical froglike behavior as long as it is exposed to light. A small male that John loaned me one summer stubbornly refused to stir until all lights were extinguished each night around midnight, when it was too dark—and I was usually too sleepy—to observe its behavior.

When John released a dozen male and female red-eyes in the greenhouse adjoining his studio, he found that darkness, potted palms and ferns, high humidity, and a shallow pool of water offered all the essential requirements for breeding. After several weeks in residence, the males began to sound their raucous mating calls just after dusk. These ordinarily slow-moving frogs would then jump from leaf to leaf, raising up their bodies and quivering excitedly. Any movement by another frog (or nearby human) would attract the attention of a male, who would chase the intruder and sometimes wrestle or pin down a competitor.

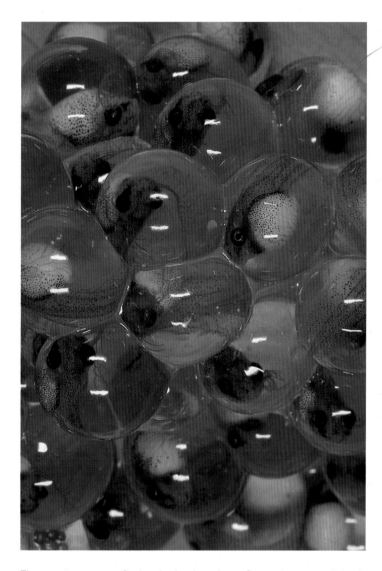

The prominent eyes of unhatched red-eyed tree frog embryos are distinctly visible when viewed closely.

When a female would begin to descend from her sleeping place, two or three males would often clasp her simultaneously and wait for her to select a suitable leaf or stem on which to lay her eggs. Eventually, one male would remain on her back long enough (sometimes twenty-four hours or more) to fertilize all her eggs. The female would attach her eggs to the underside of a leaf overhanging the water,

A developing red-eyed tree frog tadpole, sporting arms and legs, is reflected on the surface of a pond.

and, after depositing each clutch, she would climb down and enter the water to refill her bladder. Each descent to water would attract the attention of other males, who would then swarm over her and her current mate, still clasped to her back.

The eggs of the red-eyed tree frog develop rapidly. After about five days, the tiny tadpoles, now visible in their embryonic sacs, wash down the leaf into the water below when their egg sacs rupture. (Tadpoles that aren't flushed immediately into the water can flip themselves with their tails until they are able to launch themselves off the leaf.) Within a few days of being moved from the shallow pool in the greenhouse into a glass aquarium, the tadpoles would sprout slender hind legs, followed by front legs. Shortly thereafter, the tiny brown tadpoles would begin to crawl right up the sides of the glass and, in another day or two, begin to turn green and absorb their tails into their new frog-shaped bodies.

One-week-old red-eyed tree frog siblings display variation in skin color as they rest on a vine.

Frog Lore

Frogs and toads have always been something of a mystery to humans. Today, encounters with frogs seem nearly unavoidable—in popular culture, zoos, museums, and the environment around us—but our ancestors had frequent encounters, too. Amphibians, after all, were the first vertebrates to invade the land, and frogs "probably fathered all of the vertebrate music on earth," nature writer Edward Hoagland points out. One reason frogs have been such an enigma is their peculiar ability to change from one life form (the larva) to another. Some ancient societies saw this transformation as an omen and worshipped frogs for their mystical powers; others, however, regarded them as harbingers of bad fortune.

To the Egyptians, frogs were a symbol of fertility. Egyptian women wore gold amulets with depictions of frogs, hoping to incur the gods' favor of fruitfulness. And in Egyptian tombs, embalmed frogs were laid to rest beside human mummies. In Asian cultures, however, frogs and toads were believed to be a sign of bad luck. A wrinkled toad, for example, was said to be the incarnation of an ugly or evil old man, and when the "toad in the moon" (what we refer to as the "man in the moon") managed to swallow itself, the result was an eclipse. To Australian aborigines and North American Indians, the croaking of frogs was a portent of rain, and on occasion Americans and Europeans reported that the heavens "rained" frogs (which were transported, scientists speculate, by tornadoes or waterspouts that sucked up the frogs and dumped them miles from their place of origin). Then, too, the sudden appearance of a "plague" of frogs or toads, emerging in all likelihood from underground burrows after a heavy downpour to mate in temporary pools of rainwater, also fueled claims that these animals were "descending" from the skies.

In Shakespeare's day, people believed that the glittering eyes of frogs and toads betokened a precious jewel, or "toad stone," within the animal's head; if worn, one of these "stones" purportedly would protect the wearer from poisons and other evils. Europeans also believed that if someone placed a frog's tongue on the head of a sleeper, it could induce that individual to talk in his or her sleep. To predict changes in

The common names of many frogs refer to distinctive physical characteristics. This Solomon Islands leaf frog has hornlike protuberances over its eyes that resemble leaves.

weather, the Germans sometimes placed European tree frogs in glass jars with water and tiny wooden ladders. "On days when the weather will be bad, the frog stays in the water and croaks," explained a weather expert. "But as he senses clearing weather, he ascends part way up the ladder, and during ultra-fine weather, he is said to be found most often at the top of the ladder."

The green frog is sometimes called the "screaming frog" because young green frogs utter a startling, frightened scream when alarmed.

Witches, shamans, and scientists have all been drawn to the unusual features of frogs and toads. The "weird sisters"—or witches—in Shakespeare's *Macbeth* chant about "eye of newt and toe of frog" as they stir the boiling, bubbling contents of their cauldron. Witch doctors and shamans of the Amazon sometimes spike foods with skin secretions from frogs to induce trances. For centuries, the Chinese have recognized the medicinal properties of certain toads and frogs and have prescribed dried toadskins to increase a patient's low blood pressure.

During the eighteenth century, while experimenting with frogs, Italian physicist Luigi Galvani discovered that muscles can be stimulated by direct electric current. Cloning experiments with the cells of frog eggs date back to the late-nineteenth century, and adult frogs were successfully cloned in the 1960s, three decades before Scottish geneticists cloned Dolly the Sheep. In the 1940s, scientists injected African clawed frogs with urine from pregnant women and discovered that frogs could be reliable indicators of human pregnancy. And generations of students around the world have studied internal anatomy by dissecting frogs in high school and college biology classes. Approximately seven million vertebrates—mostly bullfrogs and leopard frogs—are dissected every year in the United States alone, according to the Humane Society, despite the fact that CD-ROMs and Web sites now offer "virtual frogs" to instructors and students, eliminating the need to slice open preserved specimens.

The unusual glandular secretions of toads make these animals especially tantalizing to medical re-

Toxic skin secretions from Phyllobates vittatus *and other dart-poison frogs are studied by medical researchers for possible use in treating human illnesses.*

searchers and toxicologists. The toad is "a movable drugstore," authority Robert De Graaf once remarked, "a veritable chemical factory." For example, a compound called serotonin, found in the glandular secretions of cane toads, causes blood vessels to contract and may provide medical science with treatments for heart disease, cancer, mental illness, and allergies. And the skin secretions of certain Australian tree frogs contain peptides that kill bacteria, resist viruses, and can be used to treat patients with schizophrenia. A peptide from the bicolored tree frog of South America may be able to treat depression, stroke, and Alzheimer's disease, and a toxic extract from the skin of the phantasmal dart-poison frog (*Epipedobates tricolor*) of Ecuador may lead to development of a painkiller 200 to 700 times more potent than morphine. Recently, substances synthesized from the genes of the African clawed frog have been touted as a possible weapon in the fight against an Asian fungus that has devastated American chestnut trees.

Millions of North American bullfrogs are dissected in biology classes every year, and others are cooked and served in gourmet restaurants.

Of particular interest to pharmaceutical companies are antimicrobial polypeptides called magainins, which are secreted by the African clawed frog. Synthetic derivations of these compounds, which kill bacteria by rupturing their cell membranes, are currently being tested as possible treatments for skin cancer, colon cancer, stomach infections, foot ulcers, and eye wounds, and as possible barriers to sperm and disease pathogens such as the human immunodeficiency virus (HIV).

Of course, the skin secretions of frogs and toads are not their only "contribution" to mankind. Humans regard frogs as delicacies and have happily eaten them for centuries. Every year, Americans import some 1,000 to 2,000 tons of frog legs, and the French—whom British soldiers nicknamed "Frogs" during World War I because of their appetite for these amphibians—consume an estimated 3,000 to 4,000 metric tons of frog legs annually. Overcollection of frogs in several Asian nations, for domestic consumption as well as overseas export, has resulted in alarming increases in insect populations—including flies, grasshoppers, Japanese beetles, earwigs, cucumber beetles, and cutworms—which have devastated agricultural crops and forced governments to limit or ban the sale of frogs. In Africa, decreases in frog populations have been linked to increases in cases of malaria, which is spread by mosquitoes that are eaten by frogs. To illustrate the profound impact frogs can have on insect control, researchers estimate that 1,000 tiny cricket frogs in a single pond in the Eastern United States consume approximately 4.8 million arthropods per year.

Although gray tree frogs are sometimes kept as pets, their skin secretions can irritate human eyes.

The American appetite for frog legs has waxed and waned over the years; during the California Gold Rush, in the mid-1800s, wealthy San Franciscans acquired a taste for expensive French cuisine, and restaurants slaughtered hundreds of thousands of California red-legged frogs, then began importing bullfrogs to meet the local demand. (Escapees from a frog farm across the bay from San Francisco established California's first resident bullfrog population.) In the 1950s, bullfrog farming became popular again, and the state of Florida published a how-to book for entrepreneurs that included fifty recipes for cooking frogs, among them bullfrog pot pie, bullfrog à la king, bullfrog omelet, bullfrog salad, and bullfrog clubhouse sandwich.

While some people pour sauces over their frogs, others pore over tales of their fabulous deeds. From the fables of Aesop to Mark Twain's "The Celebrated Jumping Frog of Calaveras County," frogs have popped up repeatedly in literature. Classic German and Russian fairy tales such as "The Frog Prince" and "The Frog Princess" feature frogs, and children's authors Joel Chandler Harris, Beatrix Potter, and Thornton W. Burgess, among others, have created frog characters in their stories for young readers. The conceited Mr. Toad commands center stage in Kenneth Grahame's *The Wind in the Willows,* and a host of feisty frogs and rowdy toads are familiar to youthful fans of Arnold Lobel's *Frog and Toad Are Friends* (and its sequels),

Donald Elliott's *Frogs and the Ballet*, Jane Yolan's *Commander Toad in Space*, Jim Henson's Kermit the Frog stories, and David Wiesner's fanciful *Tuesday*. Other pop-culture amphibian heroes include Frogger, Flumpa the tree frog, Gilbert de la Frogponde, Flip the Frog, and the Tijuana Toads.

Not surprisingly, even the *New York Times* has taken notice. "Frogs have improbably attained a rank of animal celebrity," the *Times* reported not long ago. Just browse the Internet for Web sites with frog subjects if you aren't convinced. Or visit the Frog Fantasies Museum in Eureka Springs, Arkansas; the Frog's Leap Vineyard in Rutherford, California ("Time's fun when you're having flies!" reads their motto); the annual Frog Festival in Rayne, Louisiana (the self-proclaimed "Frog Capital of the World"); the Calaveras County Fair and Jumping Frog Jubilee in Angel's Camp, California; or the annual Toad Suck Daze festival in Conway, Arkansas.

The ubiquitous frog really does seem to be just about everywhere nowadays—except, perhaps, where nature intended it. The signs of their population declines—and, even worse, their extinctions—should be taken seriously, and concerned citizens need to assume a more active role in amphibian conservation efforts. Indeed, anyone worried about the current disappearance of frogs would do well to contemplate the words of the narrator of T. Coraghessan Boyle's 1991 short story "Hopes Rise," after he learns about threats to frog populations while attending a herpetology convention with his girlfriend.

"What kind of world would it be without them?" he asks himself. Neither he nor anyone else knows the answer, of course—and I hope no one is ever forced to find out.

A tiger-striped monkey frog (Phyllomedusa hypocondrialis) displays the flash colors on its flanks and legs that make it popular among collectors.

Frogs in Peril

Since publication of our earlier book about frogs in 1995, photographer John Netherton and I have been saddened by many new reports chronicling the plight and decimation of frog populations around the globe, including the discovery of deformed frogs not far from where we live in Tennessee. When I wrote that book, scientific documentation of declining amphibian populations in the United States, Europe, Central America, Australia, and Asia had been finding its way into mainstream publications for only a few years. Many experts believe the moment of reckoning came in 1989, when herpetologists who had assembled in Canterbury, England, for the first World Congress of Herpetology began informally sharing accounts of species declines in their home countries. When Martha Crump informed her colleagues about the sudden disappearance of the golden toads she had been studying in Costa Rica's Montevideo Cloud Forest Reserve, herpetologists realized they needed to collect and examine amphibian-population census data before other species followed the rare golden toad's path to extinction.

In the years that followed, scientists discovered many signs of frog declines (beyond expected population fluctuations that occur over time) in dissimilar geographical regions with different climates, and they redoubled their efforts to alert the public. Findings once reported chiefly in scientific journals now were made available to ordinary citizens in mainstream magazines, newspapers, and broadcast media. And individual citizens took it upon themselves to do something.

For example, the North American Amphibian Monitoring Program and the Frogwatch Observers in Canada enlisted volunteers to go out at night to listen for frog calls and estimate the number of individuals calling from selected breeding sites. Species such as the Yosemite toad, Houston toad, mountain yellow-legged frog, California red-legged frog, cascades frog, arroyo toad, Western spadefoot toad, tailed frog, and Northern leopard frog—all North American species whose numbers had dropped alarmingly—became the focus of greater attention as researchers endeavored to identify the causes of their declines and to protect remaining individuals.

The explanation for why frogs, toads, and other amphibians are so noticeably affected by environ-

Leopard frogs in Minnesota, Wisconsin, and other states have suffered serious population declines in recent decades as a result of pollution, pesticides, disease, and loss of habitat.

mental threats was presumed obvious: Virtually all live a double life, part terrestrial and part aquatic (at least at breeding time), and consequently are twice as vulnerable as most other vertebrates. Furthermore, unlike birds, mammals, and reptiles, they have permeable skins that absorb toxic chemicals, harmful doses of ultraviolet radiation, and other dangerous substances found in water, on land, or in the atmosphere. At

Eastern spadefoot toads are well adapted to dry regions, where they burrow underground until heavy rains lure them to the surface to breed.

the same time, their natural habitats, migration corridors, and breeding grounds are being systematically destroyed. Wetlands and swamps are drained, waters dammed, forests razed, breeding ponds isolated, and habitats eliminated, to be replaced with sprawling new developments, shopping centers, industrial sites, and more roads and highways.

In short, humans are killing off the frogs—some of them directly, some of them indirectly. And the list of causes for frog declines continues to grow. In addition to habitat destruction and pollution (including sewage, toxic wastes, and metal contaminants), other causal agents have been identified: pesticides, herbicides, and fertilizers; sulfuric and nitric acids in rain and snowfall, generated by automobile exhaust; increased levels of ultraviolet-B radiation entering the atmosphere through holes in the ozone layer; nonnative predators, such as game fish and bullfrogs, introduced intentionally or accidentally; manmade endocrine disrupters that mimic or block hormones and affect sperm production and reproduction rates; overhunting of frogs for food, frog-skin products, and classroom dissections; and overcollection of live frogs for the pet trade. Climate has been found to be responsible, too (e.g., droughts, severe winters, hurricanes, global warming, and disruptive weather patterns such as El Niño), as well as

Most tadpoles, including this red-eyed tree frog larva, are highly susceptible to pesticide and fertilizer runoffs and other harmful chemicals in ponds and streams.

diseases caused by viruses, bacteria, and fungi. Some scientists believe that a combination of several factors induces high rates of mortality.

"We are convinced that declines … are real and that many of the declines have been catastrophic," herpetologists Robert Stebbins and Nathan Cohen conclude in their thorough 1995 review of sometimes-conflicting scientific literature. Amphibians, they declare, "may be in the vanguard of decline." Like the canaries taken into coal mines to detect subtle but lethal fumes imperceptible to humans, frogs are championed as "bioindicators"—that is, early heralds of an unsafe environment—thanks to their acute sensitivity to contaminants and stresses.

Golden mantellas and other species native to Madagascar are seriously threatened by widespread destruction of the island's once-plentiful rain forests.

Just as declining amphibian populations were becoming a subject of public interest, something very peculiar happened. In 1995, schoolchildren on a field trip in Minnesota noticed deformed frogs in a farmer's pond and showed the freakish-looking specimens to public health officials. The media published stories, and scientists attempted to pinpoint the cause of the deformities. As the research continued, deformed frogs began to surface in other states as well; to date, more than thirty states and at least three Canadian provinces have reported unusually high numbers of deformed frogs.

Scientists have offered several explanations. According to one early hypothesis, a microparasite common to reptiles is responsible. Another more widely accepted hypothesis suggests that excessive amounts of vitamin A compounds called retinoids cause the birth defects. Researcher Martin Ouellett, who has examined nearly 30,000 frogs along a 150-mile stretch of the St. Lawrence River valley over a seven-year period, has concluded that agricultural chemicals—chiefly methoprene and other pesticide runoffs—have triggered the abnormalities.

Recently, field researchers in Panama and Queensland, Australia, have discovered a new cause of frog die-offs: a previously unknown chytrid fungus found in sick and dead frogs that were collected in pristine rain forests. DNA analyses have since found the same fungi in captive and wild frogs elsewhere, including the United States.

To monitor and disseminate the research of international teams of scientists studying the epidemic of frog deformities and die-offs, the Declining Amphibian Populations Task Force publishes a monthly newsletter, *Froglog*, which is also available online. The data, analyses, and conclusions offered in *Froglog* and other publications help to raise public awareness and build consensus among researchers, while signaling to citizens around the world that greater efforts must be made if we genuinely wish to protect frogs and their habitats for future generations. In early 1999, a U.S. Task Force on Amphibian Declines and Deformities unveiled a new program called Frog Force, which features a Web site (www.frogweb.gov) to gather information from volunteers of all ages who encounter malformed amphibians in the wild.

Mining interests currently pose a threat to the Okefenokee Swamp in Georgia and Florida, where draining the swamp's waters will have a detrimental impact on wildlife and habitat.

Gallery of Frogs

Tree Frogs

A large assemblage of frogs is called a congress, and the resemblance of such a gathering to the U.S. Congress is striking: While the voices of individuals can be pleasing to the ear, the cacophony created by too many voices clamoring at once can be ear-piercing and shrill. Some of the most vociferous anuran (frog) offenders are the tree frogs—which can be as slippery and spellbinding as any seasoned politician.

In truth, every tree frog I have welcomed into my own home, including specimens from North and Central America, Australia, and China, has won me over. These tree frogs have all been gentle, delicate, alert, and—with the exception of the red-eyed tree frog that never stirred before midnight—enormously entertaining. Their intelligent expressions, beautiful colors, lithe bodies, and physical grace may explain their popularity as pets and help to dispel the common stereotype of frogs as plump, lumpy creatures with the brains of animatronic animals in beer commercials.

Despite their name, not all tree frogs are arboreal, although long limbs and well-developed suction disks on their toes certainly make climbing trees and balancing on branches and leaves easy. Many species, including the North American green tree frog, Australian green tree frog, European tree frog, Pacific tree frog, pine barrens tree frog, Chinese emerald tree frog, red-eyed tree frog, and scores of others, are clad in some shade of green—the ideal color for camouflage in trees and shrubs. But other tree frogs and their allies (which include spring peepers, chorus frogs, and cricket frogs) are brown, tan, gray, blotched, or spotted—dark colors and patterns more suitable for life on (or below) the ground. Some tree frogs can even alter the color of their skin, depending on such variables as the color of their background, the temperature, humidity, and their mood.

The bright skin colors, vivid eyes, long limbs, and alert expressions of red-eyed and other tree frogs contribute to their popularity as pets.

Tree frogs constitute one of the larger families of frogs (Hylidae), represented by more than 770 species in some 40 genera. The largest genus, the so-called "true" (hylid) tree frogs, includes many North American species, such as the **green tree frog,** also known as the rain frog, bell frog, cowbell frog, Carolina tree frog, and fried bacon frog. Herpetologists and pet owners consider this one of America's most

The skin coloration of individual green tree frogs can vary considerably, from bright apple green and olive to brown and even black.

beautiful frogs, and for good reason: The skin is bright apple green (though it can quickly change to dark olive, brown, or black); the eyes are gold or bronze, with striking vertical pupils; and a dashing ivory or yellow stripe runs along the upper lip and often extends along the side of the body. Long hind legs and large suction disks on the toes make this frog an expert climber.

An industrious insect-catcher, this Southern species is frequently spotted at night clinging to window screens, snatching bugs attracted to light. Its harsh *quank-quank-quank* advertisement call, said to resemble the sound of a cowbell or the words *fried-bacon, fried-bacon, fried-bacon,* is easily recognizable, and when a congress of several hundred assembles at a breeding site near water, the ensuing din can be heard a mile or more away. In their zeal to find a mate, amorous males often engage in a good deal of elbowing and shoving, says herpetologist Doris Cochran, who once watched an entire riverbank "seethe with creative furor and a mindless obedience to an instinct that insured the continuance of the race."

Occasionally mistaken for the green tree frog are the **squirrel tree frog** and the **barking tree frog,** whose ranges overlap that of the green tree frog in Southeastern states from coastal Virginia south through Florida and along the Gulf Coast. The squirrel tree frog has a light-colored stripe similar to that of the green tree frog (though more often yellow and bordered with light brown), while the barking tree frog is dotted with dark blotches or lemon-yellow spots. The squirrel tree frog is a terrific acrobat, though its name refers not to its talent for scrambling across rooftops (and

Top: Squirrel tree frogs are fast jumpers and notoriously difficult to catch.
Bottom: Barking tree frogs can usually be identified by the presence of distinct spots on the back,
though their basic skin color can vary from green to brown.

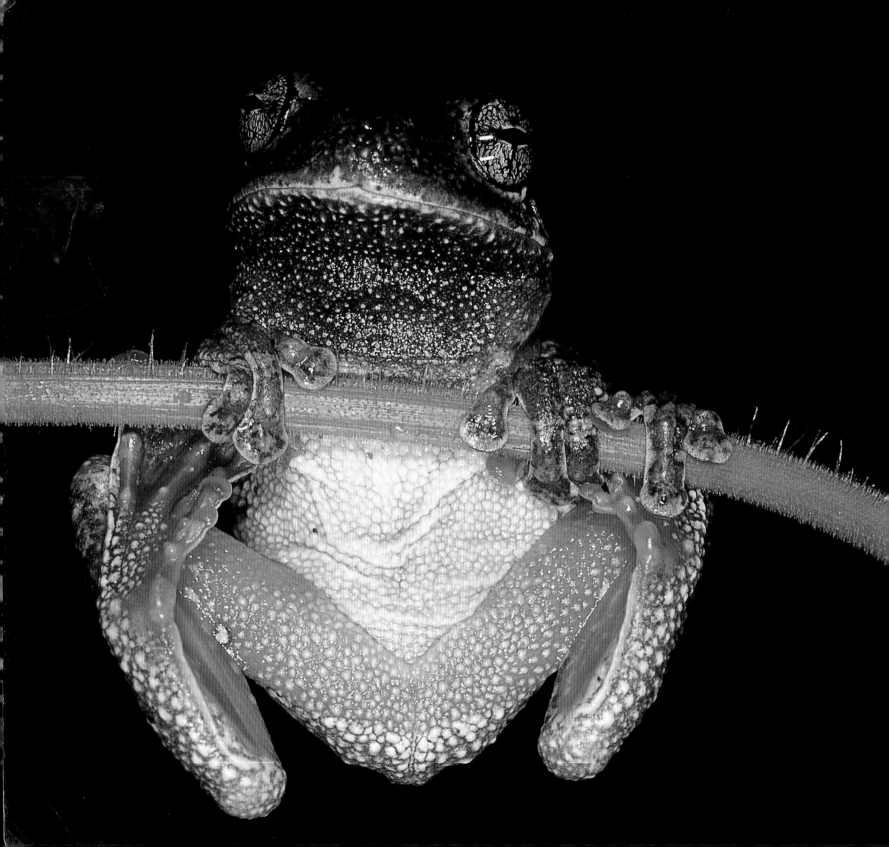

occasionally tumbling down chimneys) but to its squirrel-like chattering and its scolding rain call. (Its advertisement call, Roger Conant and Joe Collins note, sounds like "Morse code done with a snore.") The explosive *arrk-arrk-arrk* sound of a barking tree frog, on the other hand, is easily mistaken for the barking of a pack of hounds. This frog's thick, leathery skin is covered with fine granulation, and it can change in an instant to dark brown, gray, or yellow.

Despite its name, the **gray tree frog** is sometimes green, especially when still a juvenile. But typically its skin is a mottled gray with irregular markings on the back, two bars on each leg, and orange or yellow hidden on the inside of the hind legs. Overall, its rough, warty skin bears a remarkable resemblance to lichen growing on tree bark. The name of this particular frog actually refers to two lookalike species—the common gray tree frog and Cope's gray tree frog—which are difficult to tell apart unless their calls are analyzed. Both have a short, explosive trill, not unlike the bleating of a lamb, the loud purr of a cat, or the

The red-eyed tree frog is a nocturnal species that becomes active in the rain forest canopy only after sundown.

rhythmic sound of a riveter, and their ranges overlap through the Eastern United States and southern Canada. Males are aggressively territorial during the mating season, and they sometimes remain in one location for weeks, defending it from any intruder by engaging in spirited wrestling matches. While hibernating in its northern range, this frog is able to withstand temperatures as low as −20° F by producing a reserve supply of glycerol in its blood, which functions like antifreeze even when the frog is partially frozen.

Perhaps the world's best-loved tree frog—certainly the most widely photographed—is the **red-eyed tree frog** of Central America. With prominent blood-red eyes and glorious neon-green skin, accented with blue flanks and bright-orange toes, this frog has been featured on the covers of books,

Opposite: Like other tree frogs, the gray tree frog has well-developed suction disks on its toes that make climbing and balancing easy.

magazines, calendars, greeting cards, travel brochures, as well as a vast assortment of T-shirts, caps, sleepwear outfits, boxer shorts, toys, puzzles, craft items, credit cards, umbrellas, and even shower curtains. Ranging from Mexico southward into Panama and Costa Rica, this strictly nocturnal species lives in tropical rain forests, where males can be heard sounding their short *chock-chock* advertisement call or *cluck-cluck-cluck* rain call from leafy canopies near water. After mating, females attach their egg clutches to leaves that hang over the water; later, when the egg membranes rupture, the tiny tadpoles slide into the water below. Adult frogs average about 3 inches (7.5 cm) from nose to vent, which does not include their long, matchstick-thin hind legs.

Grasping a pair of reeds with its sticky toe pads, an Indonesian White's tree frog secures a firm grip while searching for insect prey or a place to rest.

Another popular tree frog is the White's tree frog of Australia and New Guinea, named for an eighteenth-century explorer. This plump tree frog is easily recognized by its rolling folds of waxy bluish green skin, which have earned it the dubious nickname "dumpy frog." (In captivity, these tree frogs are prone to overeat and grow surprisingly rotund.) In Australia, White's tree frogs are frequently encountered on verandas and inside houses (bathrooms are popular), where they thrive on a diet of crickets, cockroaches, beetles, and moths. By nature placid and easily tamed, some will readily accept food offered by humans. Both males and females have throaty voices and produce a distinctive *wark-wark-wark* call. Researchers have discovered compounds in skin secretions of the White's tree frog that can fight viruses and bacteria, lower human blood pressure, and help in the diagnosis of gall bladder and pancreatic disorders. If these compounds can be synthesized and replicated in quantity, they may prove to be enormously beneficial to the medical community.

The **spring peeper** is a tiny ally of the true tree frogs and a member of a related subfamily. Found throughout the Eastern United States and southeastern Canada, the spring peeper averages just 0.75 to 1.5 inches (19 to 38 mm). Males are well known for their familiar high-pitched *pe-ep, pe-ep, pe-ep* advertisement call, which they sound in early spring. From a distance, a chorus sounds like the jingle of sleigh bells; up close, these tiny frogs produce a deafening din. On one occasion, the shrill voice of a single male peeper that I had surreptitiously quartered in my room at a Kentucky lodge resounded so loudly that it threatened to rouse the sleeping guests next door—and I had to release it almost immediately.

Spring peepers are tiny North American frogs that can be identified by an X-shaped mark on their back.

Spring peepers emerge very early in the spring from hibernation sites in forest debris, where they ward off the effects of freezing temperatures by manufacturing glucose. These gregarious "explosive breeders" sport prominent X-shaped crosses on their brown, gray, or fawn-colored back, making identification easy. The male's vocal sac is transparent, inflating and deflating like a soap bubble or miniature balloon as it pumps air rapidly back and forth across the vocal cords. According to researchers, female spring peepers apparently favor older males, which call at a faster rate than their smaller, younger competitors.

"True" Frogs

The so-called "true" frogs, members of the genus *Rana*, belong to a large family of about 650 species, represented on every continent but Antarctica. True frogs, whose members include the North American bullfrog, leopard frog, pickerel frog, wood frog, and gopher frog, have similar bodies: head somewhat pointed, long legs, webbed feet, and smooth skin.

Bullfrogs are imposing, stout-bodied frogs with a large tympanum behind the eye and a distinct fold of skin curving behind the tympanum. Their skin color is typically green on top, spotted with dark gray or brown, and whitish on the underside (the male's throat is often yellow). Bullfrogs are celebrated for their voracious appetite, devouring practically anything they can cram into their mouths. Their diet consists primarily of insects and other invertebrates, but they also have been known to eat snakes, turtles, frogs, small birds, and even hatchling alligators. The bullfrog is North America's largest native frog, reaching a record length of 8 inches (20.3 cm), not including the legs. (One jumbo-sized "freak" specimen caught in 1949 reportedly weighed a record 7 lb. 4 oz., or 3.25 kg.)

Bullfrogs are aquatic creatures, preferring to sit perfectly still in the water near the edge of a pond, where their cryptic skin coloration provides excellent camouflage. Dominant males lay claim to a circular territory roughly 6 to 20 feet (1.8 to 6.1 m) in diameter and challenge other males that trespass, often locking together and wrestling. On the fringes, just outside a vocalizing male's territory, can be seen "satellite males," optimistically waiting to intercept females lured by the resident male. The deep-pitched call of the bullfrog resonates from two internal vocal sacs in the pouch of the throat, sounding forth a loud *jug-o'-rum, jug-o'-rum* or *be drowned, be drowned*, or *better go round*. The call is sometimes triggered by non-frog sounds, such as airplanes and chainsaws, and one memorable male responded to a women's chorus rehearsing in Florida.

Unlike the larvae of most species, bullfrog tadpoles take an unusually long time to develop into frogs, often up to two years. These jumbo-sized tadpoles feed on underwater plants and also scavenge for dead fish and other decomposing creatures. The adults are content to sit for hours at a stretch without moving

The bullfrog, North America's largest native frog, has powerful hind legs that make it an impressive jumper and strong swimmer.

but, if threatened, are capable of leaping astonishing distances. If you manage to sneak up on a bullfrog and catch it before it jumps, you may find your prisoner "playing dead" like a possum, waiting for an opportune moment to spring back to life.

Bullfrogs are highly prized for the meat on their hind legs, and "frog farmers" have been attempting to raise these frogs for years—though seldom with much success, since bullfrogs require live food and succumb to stress and disease when kept in close quarters. Regrettably, frog-farm escapees have reproduced in the wild and significantly expanded their range. Bullfrog populations now extend from coast to coast, aggressively devouring other species of frogs found in their new habitats.

The pickerel frog sports two rows of rectangular spots on its back. Its name may derive from its use as bait in pickerel fishing or from the pickerel weeds in which it often hides.

Not quite as large as the bullfrog are the **pickerel frog** and **leopard frog,** two North American species often mistaken for one another because they both have prominent spots on their backs. The pickerel frog's spots are rectangular and arranged in two parallel rows down the back, while the leopard frog's "leopard spots" are more rounded and scattered. Young pickerel frogs have a brilliant metallic luster, with a bronze or golden shine, and orange or yellow concealed on their hind legs; leopard frogs are generally a metallic green, with a pair of conspicuous ridges or folds running down the back.

Pickerel frogs and leopard frogs often forage some distance from water in meadows and weedy areas; if startled, a leopard frog will beat a hasty retreat to water by executing a series of zigzag leaps, some up to 6 feet (1.8 m). These frogs squawk loudly when jumping to safety, presumably to warn other frogs, and, if caught, may issue a piercing scream. The advertisement call of the leopard frog sounds like a snore,

Leopard frogs are often mistaken for pickerel frogs, but the dark "leopard spots" on this species are round, not rectangular, and are irregularly spaced.

grunt, or noisy chuckle, while the advertisement call of the pickerel frog is a shorter snore that "reverberates like that of a sleeping neighbor in a Pullman," a herpetologist wrote half a century ago. The pickerel frog's best protection is a toxic secretion that is highly distasteful to snakes and other predators but also has a deadly effect on other frogs housed in the same jar or container.

The male wood frog is smaller than the female. During amplexus, the male clasps the female from behind to fertilize her eggs.

Like both the leopard and pickerel frog, the **wood frog** has a prominent pointed nose, but this species is smaller and sports a handsome chocolate brown (or fawn, tan, or slightly pinkish) skin coloration with a dark brown or black "robber's mask" around and even through the eyes. The wood frog lives farther north than any other North American species, ranging throughout most of Canada and well into Alaska. It survives subfreezing temperatures in these northern habitats by manufacturing blood glucose in quantities up to sixty times greater than normal. Wood frogs mate in ponds and temporary pools of water even before winter ice has completely melted. Males utter their gravelly call—a snappy quacking noise that sounds like *cack-a-hack-a-hack* or *r-r-r-racket*—as they float on the water's surface. Wood frog tadpoles, unlike their algae-eating brethren, are carnivores and sometimes even nibble on the tails of siblings.

The typically plump and brownish **gopher frog,** spotted with irregular dark markings, lives in the American Southeast. Named for the gopher tortoise, whose long underground excavations provide a home for this species, the gopher frog is difficult to find by day but makes its presence known come nightfall, when large choruses produce a sound reminiscent of the "pounding surf" or the "roar of a distant outboard motor," according to Conant and Collins.

The gopher frog is named for the gopher tortoise burrows it resides in by day. Large choruses of males are said to sound like "pounding surf."

Toads

Scientists currently recognize about 400 species of toads worldwide, more than half of which are members of the genus *Bufo* and called "true" toads. Distinguishing a toad from a frog can be a sticky business, however. Most toads characteristically have a rather squat appearance, with short hind legs and dry, warty skin. But, to confuse matters, many species of toads could easily pass for frogs, and vice versa. (In the end, however, it matters very little, since, as herpetologist Thomas Tyning points out, "all toads, including spadefoot toads, are frogs.") Toads have glands that secrete toxic substances, which can irritate the mucous membranes of a predator or human handler.

The habitats of toads vary widely. Some toads live in deserts, while others are found in temperate forests and rain forests; some inhabit remote mountain heights, while others turn up in suburban backyards. Toads generally prefer to nestle into cool, damp burrows or other private retreats by day, emerging after dark in search of crickets, grasshoppers, mosquitoes, earthworms, slugs, snails, ants, and other prey. With such a laudable appetite for pests, it's no wonder that gardeners in France and other countries sometimes buy and release their own toads. One celebrated pet toad lived in a garden to the ripe old age of thirty-six before it died in an accident.

The **American toad** of the Eastern and Midwestern United States and Canada is a common species whose high-pitched musical trill resounds great distances through the night air during the springtime. When attracted to a male's trill, a female approaches and nudges her prospective mate; he responds by embracing her in the amplexus position and fertilizing her eggs. Extruded in long spirals of jelly, some of which extend 70 feet (21.3 m) or more, the eggs swell and eventually sink to the bottom of the water. Three to ten days later, as many as 12,000 tiny black tadpoles will hatch, gradually metamorphosing into an army of little toadlets, most of which are likely to fall prey to hungry predators.

When approached by an enemy, some American toads sprawl on their back and play dead. But a more effective defense mechanism is the whitish fluid they secrete from a pair of kidney-shaped parotoid glands behind the eyes. This fluid aggravates mucous membranes in the mouth of an animal that attempts to chew the toad, and it can cause a dog to collapse from paralysis of the respiratory system. Although

A pair of male American toads emerge on a warm spring night to produce long musical trills that attract nearby females.

humans persist in believing that a toad's secretions cause warts, there is absolutely no basis for this fear, since warts are caused by a virus.

The **Colorado River toad** of the American Southwest is an unusually bulky toad that grows up to 7½ inches (19 cm) in length. Its skin is smooth and leathery, described by observers as "rhinoceros-like." In addition to a pair of huge parotoid glands behind the eyes, this toad sports white warty glands on the corners of its mouth and on its legs. Secretions from the parotoid and other glands are extremely toxic, yet foolish humans sometimes goad these toads into secreting toxins, which they lick to achieve a hallucinogenic high. The parotoid glands insure that Colorado River toads have very few enemies—except, of course, humans, who have systematically destroyed much of the toad's natural habitat in southern California and Arizona. The male's weak, low-pitched voice has been described as sounding like a ferryboat whistle—a sound that, early in the twentieth century when the toads were far more numerous, was magnified to the volume of a deafening roar. Today, the toad's vocal abilities have apparently degenerated to such a degree that only a small percentage still use their voices.

The **European green toad** is a common species found throughout much of Europe and Asia; in Germany, eighteenth- and nineteenth-century violinists used to rub their fingers across the back of this toad to prevent perspiration. Sadly, these *Hausunken*, or "house toads," have been hit hard by industrial pollution of the Rhine River and its tributaries; today, German researchers report that 35 to 55 percent of European green toad tadpoles exhibit abnormalities apparently caused by the pollution.

European green toads have colorful emerald or olive green patches scattered across their cream-colored or brownish green backs, flecked with bright vermilion specks. Their gleaming eyes are the color of brass. These toads will congregate in damp cellars and can often be seen hopping down back alleys in search of food or cool, moist retreats. The male's call sounds like the chirp of a cricket or the creak of a door, though one famous British herpetologist insisted it reminded him of a London policeman's whistle.

Opposite, top: The Colorado River toad has a pair of large parotoid glands behind the tympanum that produce dangerous toxic secretions.
Opposite, bottom: The European green toad is adorned with olive and emerald green spots and flecks of reddish brown, and its eyes are often the color of brass.

The **marine** or **cane toad,** to the chagrin of many humans, has become a true citizen of the world. Originally a native of French Guiana, this corpulent toad was introduced to the islands of Martinique and Barbados, where its insatiable appetite for insect pests made it quite popular. From there it was introduced to Jamaica, then Puerto Rico, and later Australia and other continents. The marine toad was practically

sacred to the Puerto Rican sugar cane growers, who touted its impact on their economy at an international convention they hosted in 1932. A month later, a Hawaiian sugar planter collected 154 toads and shipped them back to Hawaii, where, after just a year and a half, their numbers had multiplied to more than 105,000. When 102 cane toads were sent to Australia three years later, they adapted well to their new environs, and 3,400 young toads were liberated in an experiment to control the grayback cane beetle. Unfortunately, while the toads were nocturnal, the insects weren't—and the burgeoning toad population began to hunt for other food on its evening forays. Today, millions of these crea-

When Australian cane growers imported the marine, or cane, toad to eat insect pests, the toads reproduced in such overwhelming numbers that they now pose a threat to native and domestic animals.

tures form a dark shuffling "sea of toads" at night, and roads are littered with their squashed bodies.

Cane toads, it turned out, not only liked to eat cane beetles, they also devoured birds, snakes, and other frogs; some even snacked on dog and cat food left outdoors (and, it is claimed, the occasional small household pet). Australians reacted by forming groups of "Toad Busters," armed with cricket and baseball bats for a good night's round of toad bashing. Today, these oversized toads, which can weigh as much as 3 pounds (1.35 kg) each and grow to 7 inches (17.8 cm), have spread throughout South and Central America and into southern Texas and parts of Florida. Unwelcome wherever they are found, they remain a symbol of the havoc humans can wreak on nature and on themselves when they introduce an "exotic" species to a new homeland and upset the balance of nature.

Spadefoot toads, which belong to another genus (*Scaphiopus*), are much smaller and quite tolerant of dry, desertlike habitats, where they use the sharp spades on their hind feet to dig holes in the sandy soil and then bury themselves. These toads estivate underground for long stretches of time until the arrival of torrential rains. Then something remarkable happens: Suddenly, thousands of pop-eyed little toads emerge at once, and the males begin uttering their plaintive advertisement call (which reminds some listeners of the cry of a crow, a cranky baby, or even a person vomiting). As the temporary pools of rainwater come alive with the sounds and frenzied motions of these "explosive breeders," the spadefoots scurry to fertilize or lay strings of eggs during their brief window of opportunity. The eggs hatch in about two days, and the tiny bronze tadpoles that emerge hasten to metamorphose into toadlets before the water evaporates. Sometimes, in a desperate attempt to stay alive, these spadefoot tadpoles will resort to cannibalism.

The Eastern spadefoot toad uses spadelike appendages on its hind legs to burrow underground during extended dry periods, only to emerge at the first sound of heavy rains.

The Eastern spadefoot toad, which ranges from New England to Louisiana, has strikingly beautiful eyes—brilliant gold with unusual vertical pupils. Secretions from this toad have a musty odor and trigger an allergic reaction among some humans. In Germany, the distinctive odor of the European spadefoot is responsible for the creature's nickname, the "garlic toad."

Dart-Poison Frogs

Some of the world's deadliest frogs are also its most beautiful, and there's a good reason: Their bright skin colors warn would-be predators to keep away, presumably by reminding them of previous ill-starred encounters. These so-called dart-poison frogs (also known as poison-dart, poison-arrow, or poison frogs) comprise more than 170 species, of which about 65 belong to three genera—*Dendrobates*, *Phyllobates*, and *Epipedobates*—all recognized for their potent toxins.

Inhabitants of humid Central and South American rain forests, these diurnal (day-active) frogs are especially tiny, some only one-half inch (1.27 cm) in length. (Males are usually a few millimeters shorter than females.) Dart-poison frogs are clad in an astonishing array of bold colors, including strawberry red, hot yellow, bright orange, deep blue, and vivid purple. Some frogs are a solid color, while others have dark stripes, swirls, spots, or flecks of contrasting colors. In recent years, dart-poison frogs have become highly popular subjects for study by toxicologists, who are interested in the potential benefits to humans of the poisons, and have also been embraced by pet owners, who are attracted by their novelty. Some dart-poison species, in fact, are so new to science they have not yet been given scientific or common names, and pet wholesalers admit they feel compelled to invent common names while they wait for the scientific community to assign a scientific name. (Both common names and established scientific names are used here for clarity.)

The outside world first learned of the frogs' existence in the early 1800s, when an English sea captain published an account of his travels in Colombia. While crossing the Andes, he had encountered natives who collected these unusual frogs and confined them in hollow canes for later use in hunting. When the time came to prepare a blow dart, a hunter would first torture or harass a frog by spearing it or holding it over a flame, then dip his blowgun darts into the deadly yellow liquid secreted by the agitated frog. The poison of just one frog, which could be dried and stored for up to a year, could treat as many as fifty darts

The mimic dart-poison frog (Dendrobates imitator), like many other dart-poison frogs, is highly variable in spotting patterns and colors and is easily confused with other species.

and was powerful enough to kill birds, rodents, monkeys, and even jaguars. (On occasion, these poisons were also used in waging war against human enemies.) Although estimates vary, scientists believe that the deadly toxin of one particular frog, the golden dart-poison frog (*Phyllobates terribilis*), could kill as many as ten humans.

The toxins of dart-poison frogs work quickly, attacking the nerves and muscles and causing death by respiratory or muscular paralysis. More than 200 different chemical substances, called alkaloids, have been identified in the secretions of dart-poison frogs, but until recently scientists were puzzled why so many varieties were necessary and why offspring of specimens in captivity fail to produce these toxins. Research studies now suggest that the large number of alkaloids is consistent with the multiplicity of potential enemies and that these chemical substances are derived from the frogs' diet of ants in the wild. Some of these alkaloids, researchers believe, may prove extremely valuable to medical science in their applications as muscle relaxants, cardiac stimulants, and painkillers.

One of the best-known species is the **strawberry dart-poison frog** (*Dendrobates pumilio*) of Costa Rica, instantly recognizable with its bright metallic-red back and deep-blue legs. Other colors and patterns are apparent as well, and populations in neighboring Panama may be yellow, orange, green, or blue. Males are territorial and will vigorously defend their turf from intruders. Individuals positioned near one another often call simultaneously, producing a buzzing *app-app-app* or ticking sound while vibrating their entire body.

The **blue dart-poison frog** (*Dendrobates azureus*), typically bright blue and dotted with black speckles, is found exclusively in isolated "islands" or pockets of rain forest on the southern savannas of Suriname along the Brazilian border. Females, when attracted by a male's subdued croaks, actively court their mate by nudging him and stroking his back. This handsome species is in great demand by the pet trade, though the export of specimens caught in the wild is illegal. Collectors have been known to smuggle them into European airports and sell them directly to clients waiting in passenger lounges.

*Top: The strawberry dart-poison frog
(Dendrobates pumilio) is a small species that
is generally bright strawberry red with deep-
blue arms and legs.
Right: Female blue dart-poison frogs
(Dendrobates azureus) from South America
court prospective mates by nudging a male and
stroking his back.*

Top, left: The green-and-black dart-poison frog (Dendrobates auratus) is found chiefly in Panama and Costa Rica, but some specimens have been accidentally introduced to the Hawaiian Islands.

Top, right: The harlequin dart-poison frog (Dendrobates histrionicus) is celebrated for its palette of vivid skin colors and patterns. Bright yellow spots are common, but other colors and patterns are found as well.

Right: The male phantasmal dart-poison frog (Epipedobates tricolor) engages in unusual breeding behavior, sometimes fertilizing the female's eggs after she has deposited them in a protected bower. After the eggs hatch, the male transports the tadpoles on his back to water.

The shy and highly variable **green-and-black dart-poison frog** (*Dendrobates auratus*) is found chiefly in Panama and Costa Rica, though it has also been introduced accidentally to the Hawaiian Islands. This frog is customarily a metallic green with large black oval spots, but some fifteen different color schemes have been reported. Usually glimpsed in the leaf litter of tropical forests and cocoa plantations, where rotting fruit attracts insects, these tiny 1 to 1.5 inch (25 to 40 mm) frogs are sometimes seen in trees as well. The male's high-pitched advertisement call attracts females, and after a pair touches snouts, they engage in a sportive chase before fertilizing and depositing the eggs on the ground beneath a leaf. The male remains to tend the clutch, leaving from time to time to soak up water and release it on the eggs to keep them moist. When the eggs hatch, the male transports the tiny tadpoles one at a time on his back to pockets of moisture in nearby trees.

The **harlequin dart-poison frog** (*Dendrobates histrionicus*), a resident of lowland rain forests in western Colombia and Ecuador, sports a remarkable array of colors, from chocolate brown, beige, and red to reticulated bands of yellow and black, with spots or bars of red, orange, green, yellow, or white. Males often vocalize from tree trunks or logs and wrestle vigorously with other males in defense of their territory. Females have been observed transporting their tadpoles to "vases" of water in bromeliads and depositing unfertilized eggs in the water as a food source for their offspring.

The **phantasmal dart-poison frog** (*Epipedobates tricolor*), found in both moist and dry habitats in Ecuador and Peru, generally has yellow or greenish stripes down its back on a base color that varies from cinnamon red or orange brown to black; in captivity, successive generations tend to lose their stripes. Males repeat a loud trill ("ad nauseam," according to one expert), and, after enticing a female to inspect several preselected bowers, the pair may engage in typical amplexus, or the male may wait for her to lay her eggs and then fertilize them after she departs. The alkaloids secreted by this species offer great promise as potential painkillers, many times more potent than morphine.

Individual populations of the **dyeing dart-poison frog** (*Dendrobates tinctorius*) are so isolated in small forest "islands" of Guiana that dramatic variations in skin color have evolved over time; as a result, many populations bear little resemblance to others. Some specimens are black and yellow with blue limbs, while others are green and black, or blue and black, with reticulated patterns on the side. According to legend, natives would rub concoctions made from the skins of these brightly colored frogs onto the bodies of young parrots where their green feathers had been plucked, in an effort to "dye" the new growth of feathers a different color. The male of this species often fertilizes the female's eggs after she has deposited them, and he then tends them for about two weeks. After they hatch, he transports the tadpoles on his back to water that collects in the hole of a tree.

Over the last decade, scientists monitoring the rate of destruction of tropical rain forests in Central and South America have voiced concerns about the fate of these tiny frogs, as well as nine related species of *Minyobates* and the dart-poison allies known as rocket frogs and skunk frogs. But unless concerned citizens join scientists in calling for governments to set aside rain forest land holdings as habitat preserves for tropical wildlife (including species yet to be discovered), future generations will likely miss out on opportunities to study, and derive actual benefits from, these extraordinary amphibians.

Secretions from the dyeing dart-poison frog (Dendrobates tinctorius) attack the central nervous system like the venom of a cobra, and experts say just handling this frog can be dangerous.

Index

Bibliography and Recommended Sources

Badger, David P. *Frogs*. Photographs by John Netherton. Stillwater, Minn.: Voyageur, 1995.

Carr, Archie. *A Naturalist in Florida: A Celebration of Eden*. Edited by Marjorie Harris Carr. New Haven, Conn.: Yale University Press, 1994.

Carr, Archie, and Coleman Goin. *Guide to the Reptiles, Amphibians, and Freshwater Fishes of Florida*. Gainesville: University of Florida Press, 1955.

Cochran, Doris. *Living Amphibians of the World*. Garden City, N.Y.: Doubleday, 1961.

Conant, Roger, and Joseph T. Collins. *A Field Guide to Reptiles and Amphibians: Eastern and Central North America*. 3rd ed. Peterson Field Guide Series. Boston: Houghton Mifflin, 1991.

DeGraff, Robert M. *The Book of the Toad: A Natural and Magical History of Toad-Human Relations*. Rochester, Vt.: Park Street, 1993.

Dickerson, Mary. *The Frog Book*. New York: Dover, 1969 (originally published 1906).

Grenard, Steve. *Medical Herpetology*. Pottsville, Pa.: N G, 1994.

Hunt, Joni P. *A Chorus of Frogs*. San Luis Obispo, Calif.: Blake, 1992.

Phillips, Kathryn. *Tracking the Vanishing Frogs*. New York: St. Martin's, 1994.

Porter, George. *The World of the Frog and the Toad*. Philadelphia: J. B. Lippincott, 1967.

Smith, Malcolm. *The British Amphibians and Reptiles*. 4th ed. London: Collins, 1969.

Stebbins, Robert C. *A Field Guide to Western Reptiles and Amphibians*. 2nd ed. Peterson Field Guide Series. Boston: Houghton Mifflin, 1985.

Stebbins, Robert C., and Nathan W. Cohen. *A Natural History of Amphibians*. Princeton, N.J.: Princeton University Press, 1995.

Tyning, Thomas F. *A Guide to Amphibians and Reptiles*. Stokes Nature Guide. Boston: Little, Brown, 1990.

Wright, Albert H., and Anna A. Wright. *Handbook of Frogs and Toads of the United States and Canada*. New York: Comstock, 1949.

Zweifel, Richard G. "Frogs & Toads." In *Encyclopedia of Reptiles and Amphibians*. 2nd ed. Edited by Harold G. Cogger and Richard G. Zweifel. San Diego: Academic, 1998.

About the Author and Photographer

Photograph © Rob Hoffman

John Netherton (left), a nature photographer for more than thirty years, lives in Nashville, Tennessee, and is the father of three sons, Jason, Joshua, and Erich. His work has appeared in *Audubon, Natural History, National Wildlife, Nikon World, Popular Photography, Birder's World,* and *WildBird,* and he writes a column for *Outdoor Photographer.* His books include *Radnor Lake: Nashville's Walden; A Guide to Photography and the Smoky Mountains; Florida: A Guide to Nature and Photography; Tennessee: A Homecoming; Big South Fork Country* (with Senator Howard Baker); *At the Water's Edge: Wading Birds of North America; Tennessee Wonders: A Pictorial Guide to the Parks; Of Breath and Earth: A Book of Days; Tennessee: A Bicentennial Celebration;* and *Frogs* (Voyageur Press, 1995) and *Snakes* (Voyageur Press, 1999), both with David Badger.

David Badger (right) lives in Franklin, Tennessee, with his wife, Sherry, and son, Jeff. He is a professor of journalism at Middle Tennessee State University, where he teaches magazine writing, feature writing, arts criticism, and movie history. He is a former film critic for WPLN-FM Public Radio in Nashville and a former book critic and columnist for the Nashville *Tennessean.* He grew up in Wilmette, Illinois, and received his A.B. degree from Duke University, M.S.J. degree from Northwestern University, and Ph.D. from the University of Tennessee. He is the author of *Frogs* (Voyageur Press, 1995) and *Snakes* (Voyageur Press, 1999), both of which were illustrated with photographs by John Netherton. He has also edited seven natural history and photography books by John Netherton.